History of Zombies

By Romero Curtiz

Minute Help Press

www.minutehelpguides.com

Table of Contents

Introduction

Zombies have spread through modern movies, literature, and comics like the apocalyptic plague they are. They fill every niche: today you can find zombies in serious horror movies, romantic comedies, and even classic works of fiction. In barely more than 40 years since their first sudden rise to popularity, zombies have risen from the dead to practically take over creative story telling.

How popular are zombies today? The Internet Movie Database (IMDb) lists over 600 full-length films featuring zombies—over 200 of them released in just the last 5 years[i]. Although Zombies remain most popular in films, they've also recently reached the number three spot on the New York Times bestselling books list with *Pride And Prejudice And Zombies* (2009), a re-imagining of Jane Austen's famous 1813 novel.[ii]

Another New York Times bestselling book, *World War Z: An Oral History of the Zombie War* (2006), has recently been turned into a screenplay by *Babylon 5* creator J. Michael Straczynki, and Brad Pitt has signed on to play the lead role.[iii] Brad Pitt in a zombie film? It could hardly have been imagined a decade ago.

But as zombies become more popular, they're also evolving. Recent films like *28 Days Later* (2002) feature faster, smarter zombies with an increased appetite for human flesh. Many recent depictions of zombies also show them not as re-animated dead but as people infected with a peculiar disease or parasite, moving further and further from the origins of zombies as undead Haitian slave labor.

Zombies have also escaped the confines of the horror niche to feature in many other genres. *Zombieland* (2009) and *Shaun of the Dead* (2004) are two comedy movies that feature romance, of all things, amid a zombie apocalypse.

Although zombies appeared on many TV shows during the 1990s and early 2000s, they almost always appeared for only one or a few episodes. For example, zombies appear in two *Buffy the Vampire Slayer* episodes. But in 2010, zombies finally got their first full-length TV series, *The Walking Dead*, which airs on the American Movie Channel (AMC) and has been renewed for a second season.[iv]

The slow, shambling walk of zombies from ancient African legend to modern horror and comedy is retraced below.

Nzambi, Zombi, and Zombies—Oh, My

"After the person [has] been buried, the act shall be considered murder no matter what result follows." — Haitian Penal Code, article 246

During the 17th and 18th centuries, thousands of Africans were captured and brought to the Caribbean islands. Forcibly exposed to the Catholic Christian religion of their capturers, yet attempting to hold onto the religion of their native lands, the captives synthesized a religion called Voodoo.

Voodoo is most strongly associated with the island nation of Haiti[v], the first nation in Latin America that freed itself from its colonial overlords. The successful slave revolution of 1804 gave Haitians the ability to practice Voodoo in the open, without having to hide it from their slave masters. This let Voodoo grow into a full-fledged and unique religion practiced today by over 10 million people in Haiti, Cuba, the Dominican Republic, The United States (particularly Louisiana), and Canada (home to a large number of Haitian expatriates).

Voodoo, which emphasizes honor and virtue like many other religions, has often been confused with its folk practices—sometimes called Hoodoo. For example, people in Haiti often nail crude puppets to trees so the living can send messages to their dead relatives—a very different purpose than the popular portrayal of sticking needles in Voodoo dolls to hurt or control the living.

Journalists and other non-scientists traveling in Haiti often sent back reports that confused Hoodoo with Voodoo, including a 1937 report by American novelist Zora Neale Hurston that told the story of Felicia Felix-Mentor, a 29 year-old woman who had died in 1907 yet apparently arose from the dead in 1936 and walked to her family home where she was identified by her siblings and husband. The woman was brought to a hospital and interviewed by a doctor who wrote:

Her occasional outbursts of laughter were devoid of emotion, and very frequently she spoke of herself in either the first or the third person without any sense of discrimination. She had lost all sense of time and was quite indifferent to the world of things around her.

This actual case was mixed with Haitian legends about "zombi" — dead people resurrected by medicine men (not Voodoo priests) who were used by rich landowners to farm their fields at night. Any farmer who profited in a bad season, it was reasoned, must be using zombies.

How Zombies Work

According to legend, a dark Voodoo wizard called a bokor finds his victims while they're still living. The bokor uses dark magic to trap the victim's soul (called an astral) in a bottle. Without a soul, the victim will soon grow weak and die.

After the victim is buried, the bokor opens the grave, calls the victim's name three times, and waves the bottle containing the astral under the person's nose just long enough to revive the body. Once revived, the victim—now a zombie—is forever under the control of the bokor.

The bokor no longer needs the bottle containing the zombie's astral, but he can use it to enhance his power—or he can sell it to someone else. Captured astrals are believed to bring luck, healing, and profit.

In Hoodoo, zombies have one weakness: feeding salt to a zombie will make it return to the grave, although the bokor can use the zombie's astral to revive it once again.

Haitians take their belief in zombies seriously. They don't want their friends and family to be revived and turned into mindless slaves, so they sometimes cut the arms or legs off of a dead person before burying him or her, or a family member guards the grave of a recently deceased person for a few weeks after death until the body decomposes enough to make revival useless.

It is not just backwater locals who take zombies seriously. Trying to turn someone into a zombie is illegal anywhere in Haiti. A translation of article 246 of the Haitian penal code reads, "It shall also be qualified as attempted murder [the causing of] a lethargic coma more or less prolonged. After the person [has] been buried, the act shall be considered murder no matter what result follows."

Are Zombies Real?

Zombies might sound like local superstition, but in 1982 a man named Clairvivus Narcisse turned up claiming to be an escaped zombie. There was a clear record of his death in a hospital on 2 May 1962 — twenty years earlier. When questioned by his friends and family, he knew answers no one else would know. His family was convinced it was him and scientists weren't able to explain how he lived.

Upon hearing about Narcisse, several scientists founded the Zombie Project, which was an attempt to explain the zombie phenomenon using scientific means and to see if zombification had any practical benefit to medical science. A Harvard ethnobotanist, Wade Davis, was sent to Haiti to investigate.

Davis discovered that Narcisse claimed that he was "conscious but paralyzed" when the doctors pronounced him dead — Narcisse even remembered his head being covered by a sheet. From this statement, Davis hypothesized that Narcisse may have been poisoned by a paralytic that mimicked death but which allowed revival.

Armed with his hypothesis and funding from a pharmaceutical research company, Davis set out to find local bokors and discover the chemical paralytic. He found that, although the locals believed magic made a person into a zombie, all of the local bokors made a formula containing tetrodotoxin (TTX) for use in the ritual that turned someone into a zombie.

In his book, *The Passage of Darkness* (1988), Davis wrote, "Tetrodotoxin turns out to be a very big molecule that blocks sodium channels in the nerves, bringing on peripheral paralysis, dramatically low metabolic rates and yet consciousness is retained until the moment of death."

Family and doctors would confuse paralysis with death, and a person would be buried alive. With a reduced metabolism comes reduce requirements for oxygen, so the paralyzed victim could survive for a few hours in their coffin until night fell and the bokor was able to retrieve their body. The bokor then needed only to wait for the poison to leave the victim's system.

Davis then explained why the victim would follow the bokor's orders: in the beginning, the bokor would use a drug that caused a state of mild hypnosis, but the bokor would enhance its effect by treating the victim as a zombie. The victim's cultural belief in zombies would reinforce the idea that they *are* a zombie and that zombies follow orders.

Zombies Come To America

"Lugosi died during production, and it shows." —
Movie critic Leonard Maltin

From 1914 through 1934, the U.S. occupied Haiti,
and soldiers returning to the United States
brought back stories about Voodoo—including
stories about zombies. Some of these stories
were published in early pulp magazines as
general fiction or horror.

Soon even people who had not heard about
zombies from Haitians were writing stories
about the undead. One of the most successful
early stories about the undead was American
horror writer H.P. Lovecraft's *Herbert West –
Reanimator* (1922). Serialized in the amateur
publication *Home Brew,* it told the story of a
scientist obsessed with cheating death.

Lovecraft said he wrote the story as a parody of Mary Shelley's *Frankenstein* (1818). The story includes several references to *Frankenstein*, including allusions to the poetry of Samuel Taylor Coleridge, an English poet Shelley alluded to in *Frankenstein*.

Herbert West – Reanimator tells the story of medical doctor Herbert West over the full course of his career, from his time in medical school, to his time as an independent practitioner, to his time in World War I, and after. West believes he can cure death using an experimental re-agent injection. He is met with constant failure — he brings people back from the dead, but they're different, more violent people.

West never takes failure as sign that he should give up, and he continues to refine his formula, testing it on one corpse after another. He meets with some success — his later victims retain more intellect than his earlier victims, but they're still violent.

The book ends as it began by parodying Frankenstein, but modern readers will find that *Herbert West – Reanimator* has a lot in common with modern zombie stories, with Lovecraft's renamiated rising out of the grave not by magic, but by science. They're cannibalistic, they form mobs, and they may portend the end of civilization.

In 1985, the book was adapted into a well-received movie, *Re-Animator*, starring Jeffrey Combs as Herbert West. Film critic Roger Ebert wrote, "I walked out somewhat surprised and re-invigorated (if not re-animated) by a movie that had the audience emitting taxi whistles and wild goat cries." Two sequels followed, *Bride of Re-Animator* and *Beyond Re-Animator*.

Other books had a significant effect on later zombie books and films. American science fiction writer and screenwriter Richard Matheson wrote *I Am Legend* (1954), a book that would later be made into three authorized and two unauthorized movies. The book tells the story of the last man left alive after a plague turns the rest of the world into apparent vampires—creatures who cannot stand daylight or garlic.

Although the monsters are labeled vampires in Matheson's book, they resemble zombies in many ways. They're not immortal, like traditional vampires, nor does the last man believe they're intelligent, as Dracula and other vampires in the Bram Stoker tradition clearly were.

It is the "last man alive" mentality affected by the main character of *I Am Legend* that influenced later zombie fiction. It is when the character uses the abandoned resources of humanity to defend himself against unthinking hordes that the connection to modern zombie films becomes most apparent.

It's also rabies-like plagues from *I Am Legend* that feature into later zombie movies such as *28 Weeks Later* (2002).

I Am Legend continues to have a lasting effect on modern horror. George A. Romero said about writing his film *Night of the Living Dead*, "I had written a short story, which I basically had ripped off from a Richard Matheson novel called *I Am Legend*."[vi] Master horror writer Stephen King said, "Books like *I Am Legend* were an inspiration to me."

Three authorized film versions of *I Am Legend* have been made. The first was 1964's *The Last Man on Earth* starring Vincent Price followed by *The Omega Man* starring Charlton Heston in 1971. A film named directly after the book was released in 2007 starring Will Smith.

But Matheson's book and the films based upon it came later. It was while the stories told by the soldiers returning from Haiti were still fresh in the minds of the public (and the screenwriters) that zombies first found their place on the silver screen. The first film clearly featuring zombies was *White Zombie* in 1932. It starred Bela Lugosi as the antagonist in one of his first major performances after 1931's wildly successful *Dracula*.[vii] The film is set in Haiti and is quite faithful to Haitian zombie legend.

The story follows Madeleine Short as she arrives in Haiti to meet her fiancé and get married. Along the way, a rich plantation owner falls in love with her and persuades Lugosi's character, Murder Legendre, a bokor, to turn her into a zombie so she will fall in love with him. Legendre poisons her to death and turns her into a zombie, but he then tries to keep her for himself. The plantation owner attempts to confront Legendre, but he discovers the bokor is turning him into a zombie as well.

When Madeleine's now-husband discovers Madeleine is missing from her grave, he too takes action against Legendre, resulting in a final confrontation between the rich plantation owner, the husband, and the evil bokor.

Although *White Zombie* received negative reviews when it was released, it made a lot of money, and modern reviewers have been less critical. Most of the criticism concerns the acting—but the movie was filmed over just 11 days, hardly giving the actors time to memorize their lines.

As the first full-length zombie film, *White Zombie's* has clearly influenced many later works. It spawned one direct sequel, *Revolt Of The Zombies* (1936), although that film received only poor reviews and was a box-office failure.

American heavy metal band *White Zombie* also takes their name directly from the movie. The lead singer of the band says, "*White Zombie* is a great film that not a lot of people know about … It amazes me that a film that is so readily available can be so lost."

Although the later 1930s would be peppered with the occasional zombie movie, the next zombie movie to win critical acclaim and large box office returns was 1943's *I Walked With A Zombie.* Although *White Zombie* influenced parts of the film, it drew the majority of its inspiration from Charlotte Bronte's 1847 book, *Jane Eyre*, starting a synthesis of classic English literature with zombie lore that continues to this day.

The director of the film received only the title of the movie from the studio — it was up to him and his team to write and produce the film. The resulting movie was, in 2007, called by *Stylus Magazine* the fifth best Zombie movie of all time.[viii]

The protagonist is Canadian nurse Betsy Connell, who is hired to care for a sick woman on a Caribbean island. The woman is strangely ill and doesn't respond to any treatment she receives from Connell. As Connell searches for the cause of the illness, she discovers Voodoo rites being practiced elsewhere on the island. The locals examine the sick woman and pronounce that she is a bloodless zombie. They demand that she be turned over to them.

The plot, the acting, and the sets were all praised by contemporary critics. The complex themes of slavery and domination and the non-stereotyped portrayal of the black characters are still praised by critics today. The film's critical success but modern obscurity has lead the makers of the *Saw* series to begin producing a remake of the film.[ix]

Unfortunately, the high standards seen in *I Walked With A Zombie* weren't applied to every zombie film. The genre probably sunk to its lowest level with 1959's *Plan 9 From Outer Space*. Although titled as a science fiction movie and featuring aliens, most of the monsters in the movie are zombies.

The plot, if it can be described as such, shows aliens who fear that humans may soon discover a doomsday weapon that could destroy the universe. In response, they institute "plan 9" to re-animate the dead in order to force people to pay attention to their message of impending universal apocalypse. (Plans 1 through 8 are never mentioned.)

The movie claims to feature Bela Lugosi as a zombie, but the film footage used in the movie was shot three years earlier for another film shortly before Lugosi died, so the director, Ed Wood, hired his wife's chiropractor to play Lugosi's character in most of the scenes while disgusting his face throughout. Movie critic Leonard Maltin would later write, "Lugosi died during production, and it shows."

It's not enough that the plot hardly makes sense; the dialogue used in the movie just doesn't work. For example, the introduction lets you know that, "future events such as these will affect you in the future." Other mistakes include the flying *saucers* being described by the narrator as "cigar-shaped," clearly-visible strings holding up the flying saucers, and an airline pilot using a candlestick-style telephone to contact the aircraft control tower.

The film's many flaws caused it to be labeled as the worst film ever made, but one modern movie guide says, "The film has become so famous for its own badness that it's now beyond criticism."[x]

By the mid–1960s, zombie films were just barely crawling out of the grave dug for them by *Plan 9 From Outer Space* when director John Giling launched them into the modern era with 1966's *Plague Of The Zombies.* Although the movie is a classic of the genre, it is best known for its effect on future films.

Set in England during the mid–19th century, a rich landowner returns from Haiti with knowledge of Voodoo. Discovering a shortage of cheap labor, he uses Voodoo to turn the unwitting townspeople into zombies, unintentionally setting off a mysterious plague among the living.

The final scenes of the movie show a murderous zombie horde similar in character to the zombie masses seen in almost all later zombie films.

Night of the Living Dead And The Zombie Apocalypse

"The kids in the audience were stunned. There was almost complete silence. The movie had stopped being delightfully scary about halfway through, and had become unexpectedly terrifying. There was a little girl across the aisle from me, maybe nine years old, who was sitting very still in her seat and crying." —Film critic Roger Ebert about *Night Of The Living Dead*

Probably the most influential zombie work of all time, George A. Romero's *Night Of The Living Dead* can be credited as creating the typical modern zombie. But Romero was influenced significantly by previous works.

He conceived of *Night of the Living Dead* as a prequel to Richard Matheson's book, *I Am Legend* (1954). That book begins a couple years after all mankind, save for one survivor, has succumbed to a plague that turns them into cannibals. Romero wanted to show want happened when the plague was new and society had just begun to collapse. Romero said:

I thought *I Am Legend* was about revolution. I said if you're going to do something about revolution, you should start at the beginning. I mean, Richard [Matheson] starts his book with one man left; everybody in the world has become a vampire. I said we got to start at the beginning and tweak it up a little bit. I couldn't use vampires because he did, so I wanted something that would be an earth-shaking change. Something that was forever, something that was really at the heart of it. I said, so what if the dead stop staying dead? … And the stories are about how people respond or fail to respond to this. That's really all [the zombies] ever represented to me.

Although Romero rejected the vampire-like elements of *I Am Legend*, he also rejected the Haitian origin of zombies—in fact, for all of its influence on later zombie films, *Night Of The Living Dead* never refers to the undead as zombies. The undead in the film are called ghouls.

An important factor in the making of *Night Of The Living Dead* was its budget. It was an independent film made by first-time filmmakers, many of who contributed their own money. Including some outside financing, the full film budget was only $112,000. This limited the entire movie to just three locations—and 90 percent of the film to just one location, a farmhouse scheduled for destruction in real life, which allowed the filmmakers to damage it during filming.

The budget also forced Romero to film on cheaper black and white film, although the classic era of black and white films was decades in the past. Many reviewers believed this worked to the advantage of the film, giving it a documentary feel.

Filming without color helped reduce other costs. For example, instead of producing fake blood, the special effects manager was able to just use chocolate syrup. Flesh and entrails seen in the film were donated by one of the actors who owned a local butcher shop—they were ham and pig entrails. Costumes came from Goodwill or were brought by the extras themselves.

But probably the most important decision made because of the budget was to make the undead dumb and slow moving. It was a decision borne out of the need to hire cheap extras with no acting skill. Of all other decisions made, it probably did the most to further the zombie genre, as a cheap extras budget would permit the creation of many more low-budget zombie films during the ensuing decades.

The story told in *Night Of The Living Dead* is fairly simple and action-oriented. Barbra and her brother drive to their father's grave, where they are attacked by a zombie, and the brother dies. Barbra flees, but she crashes her car and goes to a nearby empty farmhouse to hide. The hero of the film, Ben, arrives at the farmhouse and boards up the windows and doors to keep out the approaching zombies.

The radio and television provide some clues about what's going on: a space probe recently exploded in the Earth's atmosphere, leaking radiation and causing the recently deceased to reanimate and begin to eat the flesh of living humans. Zombies can only be killed by a gunshot or heavy blow to the head.

Barbra, Ben, and several others who have arrived at the farmhouse argue among themselves while fighting off the zombies trying to get into the house. Some of them are bit by zombies, grow sick, die, and reanimate as zombies. Some of them die from other causes, eventually leaving only Ben still alive. Like *I Am Legend*, the film concludes with a twist ending.

Although the film would go on to become one of the most profitable horror films ever made, earning over $42 million dollars out of a $112,000 budget, Romero wasn't able to find a distributor for over a year after filming finished. Two major studios offered to distribute it—if it was censored and the ending was changed—but Romero refused, saying, "none of us wanted to do that. We couldn't imagine a happy ending. Everyone want[ed] a Hollywood ending, but we stuck to our guns."

Finally a distributor was found and the only change they requested was that the original title be changed from *Night Of The Flesh Eaters* to *Night Of The Living Dead*, a change to which Romero agreed. But when the title was changed, the movie's copyright statement was accidentally removed, which under 1968 copyright law meant that the film became public domain. This helped make *Night Of The Living Dead* one of the most widely distributed films ever made — 23 companies currently sell copies of it and, to date, it is the second most downloaded feature film on the Internet.

Night Of The Living Dead was released before the MPAA movie rating system was instituted, so even young children could watch it. Film critic Roger Ebert heavily criticized those theatres that let children watch the film unattended and even suggested that parents tell their teenagers to avoid it. However, Ebert has nothing but praise for the film itself, "I admire the movie itself, which I have seen twice since that 1967 afternoon, and its sequel *Dawn of the Dead* got an enthusiastic review from me. … If I were to rate it today, I'd give it 3 [and] 1/2 stars."[xi]

Beyond the critics, film historians and social commentators have alternatively praised and criticized the film for its portrayal of contemporary issues. It has been almost universally praised for casting an African-American as the hero in a film where all the other cast members were white. Romero says race had nothing to do with his decision and that the actor who plays Ben, Duane Jones, "simply gave the best audition."

But other commentators criticized the scripted lines Romero gave to Barbra, lines which depict her as dumb, helpless, and incapable of dealing with the situation.

Other commentators read more into the film. Writer Elliot Stein of the *Village Voice* thought the film criticized American involvement in Vietnam, saying, "[the film] was not set in Transylvania, but Pennsylvania — this was Middle America at war, and the zombie carnage seemed a grotesque echo of the conflict then raging in Vietnam"

Several pundits commented on the fate of the hero (African-American Ben) in relationship to the ongoing civil rights movement of the time, in particular the then-recent assassinations of Malcom X and Martin Luther King, Jr..

Other theories about the meaning of film are perhaps further afield. Film historian Robin Wood said the film was a critique of capitalism: "cannibalism represents the ultimate in possessiveness, hence the logical end of human relations under capitalism".

Night Of The Living Dead has been remade twice. The first remake in 1990 featured Patricia Tallman of *Babylon 5* fame as Barbra, now a more active heroine. The second remake, *Night Of The Living Dead 3-D,* was not approved by Romero. Neither remake was very popular.

Five sequels followed *Night Of The Living Dead*, starting in 1978 with *Dawn Of The Dead* (titled *Zombi* in Italy and some other countries). Like *Night Of The Living Dead*, it was made on a modest budget, this time $650,000, and earned enormous returns — an estimated $55 million.

None of the original characters from the first movie return in *Dawn Of The Dead*. Instead, the film shows the breakdown of society during the zombie plague — the first film example of the now common "zombie apocalypse" theme.

The film is again set in Pennsylvania, this time around Philadelphia and Pittsburgh. The events take place several days after the start of the zombie plague as the government response proves ineffective and people begin to look out only for their own survival. The four protagonists take refuge in a mall because it has everything they think they'll need to stay alive, but as time goes by they discover that materialistic goods are worthless when you expect to be trapped for the rest of your life.

When other surviving humans realize the mall may have much-needed food and supplies, they attack the mall-dwelling protagonists with disastrous consequences.

Despite Romero's incredible success with *Night Of The Living Dead*, he also had difficulty finding funding for *Dawn Of The Dead*. Indeed, the film could only be made after an Italian director provided Romero with financing in exchange for international distribution rights. But selling the international rights did upgrade Romero's budget and let him produce a higher quality film than *Night Of The Living Dead*.

One obvious difference between the two films is that the later film is entirely in color. This, of course, necessitated a change in the fake blood used. The chocolate syrup of the original film would not make a convincing blood substitute in a color film. The fake blood chosen was a new product released by the 3M corporation — the visual effects supervisor thought it was too bright, but Romero thought it would enhance the film. Film critics have mostly agreed with Romero, but the bright, gruesome blood would cause other problems when the film was ready to be shown.

The first film made it into the theatres only because the MPAA ratings board had not yet formed when *Night Of The Living Dead* was released, but by 1977 when *Dawn Of The Dead* was in post-production, the ratings board reviewed it and gave the violent, gory film an X rating — a rating which at the time meant the film would probably only be shown in special theaters. An X rating meant the film would probably never be profitable, so Romero decided to release it as "unrated", which left the decision about who could see the film up to theater owners.

A lasting consequence of Romero's funding the film by selling the international distribution rights is the proliferation of multiple versions of the film, from the faster-paced Italian version to the watered-down German version to the almost violence-free Japanese version. DVD and Blu-ray releases of the film often contain more than one version of the film, and there are at least three commentary tracks made for different versions of the film, making the film a treasure for fans of horror and zombies.

Dawn Of The Dead met with much of the same critical acclaim, box-office success, and positive social commentary that met *Night Of The Living Dead.* Movie critic Roger Ebert gave it four out of four stars and said it was "one of the best horror films ever made… the acting performances are uniformly strong; and the script develops its themes more explicitly, with obvious satirical jabs at modern consumer society."

The Rise Of The Modern Zombie

"[What is it about zombies that resonates so strongly with Americans?] I think the survival element is VERY strong in American culture. We are a nation of individualists. We believe with the right tools and talent that we can survive anything." — Max Brooks, author of World War Z

In the early 1980s, zombie movies were still far too rare to count as an authentic sub-genre of horror films. But then they received a huge boost from an unexpected source — the King of Pop.

In late 1983, Michael Jackson's latest album, *Thriller*, had dropped out of the number one spot on the bestselling albums list, much to Jackson's dismay. He called his CBS record executive Walter Yetnikoff and said, "Walter, the record isn't number one anymore. What are we going to do about it?" Two music videos had already been made for the album, but Jackson's manager came up with the idea of making a third video — and for this video he enlisted Hollywood director John Landis, who had previously made major movies such as *The Blues Brothers*, *An American Werewolf In London*, and *Trading Places*.[xii]

No Hollywood director had ever made a music video at that time, but for a large fee Landis was persuaded to cooperate and, together with Jackson, they began to pen the script to the now-famous *Thriller* music video.

The video begins with Jackson proposing to his girlfriend before he turns into a werewolf in what's revealed to be a movie scene featuring famous horror actor Vincent Price. In apparent real-life, Jackson chases after his girlfriend as she leaves the theater in fear. As Jackson sings the theme song to the movie, Thriller, he transforms into a zombie and, with other zombies, performs one of the most famous dance numbers in music video history—a dance number Jackson worked on for weeks. Jackson later said about the rehearsals:

It was a delicate thing to work on because I remember my original approach was, 'How do you make zombies and monsters dance without it being comical?' So I said, 'We have to do just the right kind of movement so it doesn't become something that you laugh at.' But it just has to take it to another level. So I got in a room with [choreographer] Michael Peters, and he and I together kind of imagined how these zombies move by making faces in the mirror. I used to come to rehearsal sometimes with monster makeup on, and I loved doing that. So he and I collaborated and we both choreographed the piece and I thought it should start like that kind of thing and go into this jazzy kind of step, you know. Kind of gruesome things like that, not too much ballet or whatever.

Thriller was amazing popular, it is also the most profitable music video of all time—the documentary produced at the same time as the music video, called *Making Michael Jackson's Thriller*, remains the top-selling music video of all time according to the Guinness Book Of World Records for selling over a million copies.[xiii]

The enduring effect of the video can be seen in both the music and film businesses—after the release of Jackson's video, it became common to hire Hollywood directors for music videos and, in 2009, *Thriller* became the first (and so far only) music video to be inducted into the National Film Registry of the Library of Congress for being "culturally, historically, or aesthetically" significant. Thanks in large part to the success of the title track's music video, the *Thriller* album remains to this day the best-selling album of all time.[xiv]

Thriller's success also helped encourage funding for several zombie films that had been languishing in pre-production, including a film made by Romero's former associate John Russo.

In 1967, Romero worked with screenwriter John Russo to make *Night Of The Living Dead*, but Romero and Russo went their separate ways afterwards, with Russo retaining the rights to make movies with "living dead" in the title.[xv] His first film using this title was released in 1985 as *Return Of The Living Dead*.

Unlike *Night Of The Living Dead*, *Return Of The Living Dead* was a horror-comedy film. Many other things set it apart from Romero's films: zombies were created by government experiments, they move fast, and they can be quite smart. The zombies also specifically desire brains rather than just any living human flesh. Above all else, the film focuses on humor rather than the sly social commentary Romero put into his films.

The movie starts when a zombie corpse is accidentally released from containment in a medical storage warehouse. In the cemetery next door, the dead begin to rise, and (like many zombie films) the heroes must defend themselves and try to end the zombie plague before it gets out of hand.

Although the film was a minor box office success, earning only $14 million, it did well considering its budget of $4 million, and spawned four sequels to date. It's better known for influencing many later zombie films that didn't follow the Romero tradition, films that would use faster or smarter zombies, and zombies that desired brains. Indeed, the movie's most famous line has been repeated or parodied too many times to count: "Brains... more brains..."

Besides *Return Of The Living Dead*, 1985 was a huge year for zombie films. That year also saw the release of *Re-Animator*, the movie based on Lovecraft's *Herbert West – Reanimator*, and *Day Of The Dead*, Romero's sequel to *Dawn Of The Dead* and *Night Of The Living Dead*. Many less notable zombie films would follow for the next several years, including un-notable films like *Zombie Vs. Ninja*, *Zombie Death House*, and the film *Redneck Zombies*, whose greatest achievement was being mentioned on a Trivial Pursuit card.

The vast increase in zombie movies and the decline in production values (which some might say were already too low), helped create the sub-genre of zombie parody films. Although parodies are discussed later, it can be argued that the successful pioneering zombie parodies of the 1980s and 1990s broadened the market for zombie films, making possible the current flood of zombie fiction.

Although zombies and the undead were featured in many of the earliest video games, they finally came into their own with 1996's *Resident Evil* for the Playstation console. The game, also known in Japan as *Biohazard,* spawned several game sequels, four films, comics, and other adaptations, making it one of the most successful zombie franchises.

The first game begins on 24 July 1998 when a team of elite police are dispatched to investigate a series of strange murders and the disappearance of the previous investigating team. While searching for clues, they're attacked by vicious creatures, some of them zombies, and discover that people are being mutated by a genetically-modified virus called the T-virus.

The sequel games and the movies also feature zombies and other monsters created by genetic manipulation. Both the games and the movies have been huge commercial successes. The games, particularly *Resident Evil 2*, have been cited in many top–10 or top–100 best games lists. The movies have earned over $600 million — making them financially the most successful zombie movie franchise yet.

In 2002, the "fast zombies" of *Return Of The Living Dead* crossed over into serious horror in *28 Days Later*, a film set in contemporary London 28 days after the outbreak of a virus that turns people into rage-filled monsters. Called "the infected" in the film, these zombies share little in common with Romero's classic zombies — except their desire to attack the living. They're smart and fast — faster perhaps than normal people.

The story starts with bicycle rider Jim, who awakens in a deserted hospital 28 days after falling into a coma. While he laid unconscious, most of Great Britain was inflected by the "rage" virus, a rabies-like virus which infects its host almost immediately, turning them violent.

Jim encounters a few other survivors in London and together they follow the radio beacon of a group of soldiers who claim to have a cure to the plague. But, upon arriving at the military barricade, they're captured by the troops, who tell them that "the cure" is to let the infected starve to death. Worse, the all-male troops plan to use the women as breeding stock by raping them and using their offspring to re-populate the English isles. Jim, who by this point has bonded with his band of survivors, attempts to liberate the women before the worst comes to pass.

Although the writers of *28 Days Later* spurned much of Romero's zombie lore, they did credit him as an inspiration and wrote references to his works into several scenes. The rabies-like nature of the plague also harkens back to Matheson's *I Am Legend*, where it was a contagious disease that wiped out humanity rather than something mystical or mysterious.

Film critic Roger Ebert wrote, "*28 Days Later*, ... begins as a great science fiction film and continues as an intriguing study of human nature." The film was a huge success. Like many zombie movies that expect only limited success, it was filmed for cheap—only about $7 million in this case—but it earned over $82 million worldwide. Its success led directly to one sequel, *28 Weeks Later*, with another sequel likely (*28 Months Later*).

It's quite likely that the surprise success of *28 Days Later* helped make possible the transition of zombies into books. Although a few fiction titles featured zombies since Lovecraft published *Herbert West – Reanimator* in 1922, many authors found it difficult to make the slow, shambling zombies of the silver screen into terrifying monsters on the printed page. American author Max Brooks found a novel way around this dilemma.

In 2003, Brooks published *The Zombie Survival Guide*. As its title implies, it provides the reader with useful advice about how to survive zombie outbreaks small and large. It also describes actual previous zombie outbreaks during the last 60,000 years, including blaming zombies for the mysterious disappearance of the failed Roanoke Colony in 1588 or 1589.

According to Brooks, the virus Solanum creates zombies. You can catch the virus when an open wound comes in contact with blood or saliva from a zombie. A quick amputation of your limb may save you, but it probably won't. Brooks also explains the difference between fake Voodoo zombies and real solanum-created zombies.

Brooks then describes the weapons you'll need to defend yourself. This part of the book, Brooks says, took the most research, as he analyzed actual weapon specifications. Although almost any weapon will do, Brooks most strongly recommends the M1 carbine and AK–47 guns, machetes, crowbars, samurai katana swords, trench warfare spikes, and Shaolin spades.

Advice on turning buildings into effective fortifications or avoiding zombies while on the run precede a chapter about attacking zombies (which is to be avoided whenever possible). Brooks concludes his book with instructions about how to rebuild society after the collapse of civilization due to a worldwide outbreak of Solanum.

The Zombie Survival Guide was a huge success. It made the New York Times bestseller list, perhaps a first for a zombie book. Although the initial print for the book was a mere 18,000 copies, over 1 million copies have been sold by 26 October 2009[xvi]. Brooks would use the ideas expounded in the book to write a sequel.

World War Z: An Oral History Of The Zombie War (2006) collects accounts of people who survived a worldwide zombie outbreak. Brooks tells the story from the perspective of a United Nations official responsible for collecting information about how the zombie plague started and how people survived it.

Although the virus that causes zombies pre-dates history, this outbreak began in China. The Chinese government attempts to cover up the outbreak, but is ineffective at fighting it and the infection spreads to other countries. By the time the plague comes to the world's attention, it's too late to effectively stop it and the American government learns the hard way that military tactics designed to fight the living are useless against the undead.

Brooks's future history obviously criticizes present policy. For example, his characters blame American over-involvement in minor foreign affairs for the inability of the American military to effectively respond to the zombie threat. The persistent animosity between Middle East nations results in several of them destroying each other in nuclear war when the zombie plague forces them to take action.

One of the best parts of *World War Z* is Brook's description of how the world's geopolitical landscape changes because of the war. Formerly poor countries that successfully defeated the zombie plague early often come out ahead of rich nations that were unprepared to make war upon the undead.

Another issue raised by Brooks in *World War Z* is government ineptitude. Reviewer Alden Utter wrote, "Early warnings are missed, crucial reports go unheeded, profiteers make millions selling placebos, the army equips itself with tools perfect for the last war they fought, and populations ignore the extent of threat until it is staring them in the face — this is, surprisingly, a post-Katrina zombie tale."[xvii]

Brooks also uses the book as a platform to help encourage Americans to think about global issues from an international perspective. "I love my country enough to admit that one of our national flaws is isolationism. I wanted to combat that in World War Z and maybe give my fellow Americans a window into the political and cultural workings of other nations."

Zombies That Make Us Laugh

"The first rule of Zombieland: Cardio. When the zombie outbreak first hit, the first to go, for obvious reasons… were the fatties." – The character "Columbus" from Zombieland (2009)

For almost as long as there have been horror movies, there have been horror parodies. It's easy to see how fear and laughter go hand-in-hand, and when horror movies so often require us to accept the impossible or unlikely, it's easy for even novice screenwriters to turn the tables and show us how absurd monster movies really are.

But the best writers can take a horrifying idea like flesh-eating zombies and turn it into not a parody but a genuine independent work worth watching or reading on its own merits.

In 1992, director Peter Jackson (who would later go on to produce and direct the *Lord Of The Rings* trilogy) released his film *Dead Alive* (named *Braindead* internationally). One of the goriest films ever made, it's a slapstick comedy featuring zombies that pokes fun at several common horror tropes.

Hundreds of years ago, according to *Dead Alive*, rats infected with the black plague raped tree monkeys in New Zealand, producing the Sumatran Rat-Monkey whose bite can turn a person into a zombie. In the opening scene, a person bit by the rat-monkey has his hands, arms, and later head chopped off by natives after he becomes infected.

Back in civilization, a captured rat-monkey accidentally infects the mother of Lionel, the protagonist. She turns into a zombie and begins murdering other people, turning them into zombies as well. Lionel covers up for her and tries to keep her under control by sedating her, but he ultimately fails and must fight off a plague of zombies. He surprising succeeds, only to have to face his mother in a horribly campy scene that ends the movie.

The movie is best known today among fans of horror and zombies for its witty dialog, with such memorable quotes as the protagonist saying, "that's my mother you're pissing on" and a Catholic priest saying, "Stand back boy! This calls for divine intervention! ... I kick ass for the Lord!"

To get an R-rating in the U.S., over 10 minutes of footage had to be removed from the movie, but Peter Jackson's preferred version, which is unrated, is widely regarded today as a cult classic.

As slapstick-style comedy mostly fell into distaste in the late 1990s, later zombie parodies and comedies would attempt to cross genre boundaries into dramatic and romantic territory.

In 2004, actor Simon Pegg starred in the first British "romantic zombie comedy," *Shaun Of The Dead*. Pegg, best known for playing Montgomery "Scotty" Scott on the *Star Trek* reboot, plays a rudderless 29-year-old who fails at almost everything. He gets no respect at his job, his girlfriend breaks up with him, and his roommate Ed is a total loser — until one day the zombie apocalypse strikes.

Waking up hung over, Shaun and Ed must fend off zombies on their front lawn. Realizing that both his mother and girlfriend are in mortal danger from the zombies, Shaun and Ed proceed to attempt to rescue them. The rest of the movie follows Shaun's successes, failures, and his handling of a group that only knows him as a failure.

Similar to *World War Z*, one of the best parts of the film takes place six months after the action, as we see how the world dealt with the zombie plague. It's a funny look at how zombies can be put to good use.

The idea for the movie grew out of an episode the TV show *Spaced* which also featured Simon Pegg.[xviii] In the episode, Pegg's character hallucinates fighting off a zombie invasion in his dreams after playing a game of *Resident Evil 2*.

Both Pegg and the director of *Shaun Of The Dead* were huge fans of Romero's "of the dead" films, and the movie contains many references to them besides the title. Romero loved *Shaun Of The Dead* in return and offered Pegg and his co-star lead roles in his next film — they turned down Romero's offer, but both did appear in the film as minor zombies.

After earning over $30 million worldwide, the movie received wide critical acclaim. Horror writer Stephen King wrote that the movie was "a '10' on the fun meter and destined to be a cult classic." Director Quentin Tarantino said it was one of the top twenty films made since 1992. The reviewer for the BBC called the film a "side-splitting, head-smashing, gloriously gory horror comedy [that will] amuse casual viewers and delight genre fans."

Following in the footsteps of *Shaun Of The Dead* was another romantic zombie comedy film destined to become the highest grossing zombie film ever. The film, *Zombieland*, premiered in 2009 and features an America ravaged by a zombie apocalypse with only a few people left living. Although the film features romantic elements, its higher budget also let the film feature much more action as well as include a celebrity cameo.

The main character starts out on a road trip to Columbus, Ohio, to see if his parents survived the zombie apocalypse. He meets up with a hardened southerner and, eventually, two sisters. Together they travel towards an amusement park rumored to be free of zombies. Along the way, they learn the most effective ways to fight zombies and stay alive and codify what they learn as rules, which are often proven in comedic situations.

Some of the rules are, "travel light", "get a kickass partner", "avoid strip clubs", "check the back seat", "don't be a hero," and "beware of bathrooms."

They also meet Bill Murray, playing himself, disguised as a zombie so that he can play golf in peace. As they travel, romance brews between the main character and the older sister, but when they reach the amusement park and discover it's a death trap, it isn't clear who will survive.

The special effects makeup designer for *Zombieland* also worked nearly thirty years earlier to create the zombies used in Michael Jackson's *Thriller* music video. For one scene in the amusement park, he needed to makeup over 160 zombies, and he took special delight in making the most physically attractive actors look horrible.

Zombieland also borrows more from recent zombie films than the older Romero films. The director describes the zombies as "Ferocious, infected people that move erratically. They are diseased, as opposed to undead. These are not the lumbering walking dead of Romero's zombie movies, but instead the super jacked up 28 Days Later/Dawn of the Dead [remake] zombies. They are scary, gnarly, and gross."

Perhaps unsurprising, considering *Zombieland*'s status as the top grossing zombie film, it was well-received by film critics. Robert Ebert wrote, "The filmmakers show invention and well-tuned comic timing." About Bill Murray's cameo, reviewer Marc Savlov wrote, it was "the single most outrageously entertaining unexpected celebrity cameo of any film — genre or otherwise."

One reviewer at *Time* magazine compared the movie to *Shaun Of The Dead:* "Edgar Wright and Simon Pegg set a high bar for this sub-genre with Shaun of the Dead, but Reese, Werner and Fleischer may have trumped them ... This isn't just a good zombie comedy. It's a damn fine movie, period."

Just as mainstream zombie fiction crossed over into print effectively with Max Brooks's *Zombie Survival Guide*, zombie parodies were able to cross into print in 2009 with *Pride And Prejudice And Zombies* by Seth Grahame-Smith. The book is a mashup—an artistic work made out of other artistic works. In this case, Jane Austen's 1813 classic is combined with Romero-style zombies and ninja fighting to produce a surprisingly innovative work.

The idea for the mashup came from editor of Quirk Books, Jason Rekulak, who compared a list of "popular fan-boy characters like ninjas, pirates, zombies, and monkeys" with another list of public domain books. Grahame-Smith said, "[Rekulak] called me one day, out of the blue, very excitedly, and he said, all I have is this title, and I can't stop thinking about this title. And he said: *Pride And Prejudice And Zombies*. For whatever reason, it just struck me as the most brilliant thing I'd ever heard."

The mashup adheres roughly to Austin's original novel, but adds zombies and ninja fighting throughout. (The novel also mentions skunks and chipmunks, though neither are native to England, which is probably an oversight of Grahame-Smith.) Some reviewers loved it, and some hated it. *Entertainment Weekly* gave it a grade of A-. *Library Journal* recommended the novel "for all popular fiction collections." But The *New Yorker* called the combination of Austin and Grahame-Smith "one hundred per cent terrible."

Whatever the opinion of the critics, the book was a financial success. In April 2009, it was number three on the *New York Times* bestseller list and Lionsgate, a Hollywood studio, acquired the rights to make the movie.

But, although *Pride And Prejudice And Zombies* appears to be the vanguard of mashup novels, it isn't much different than 1943's adaptation of Charlotte Bronte's *Jane Eyre* into *I Walked With A Zombie*. It is an interesting coincidence that the writers of both *I Walked With A Zombie* and *Pride And Prejudice And Zombies* received their titles from other people with instructions to fill in the details.

Walk Like A Zombie

"On October 31, 2006, a young woman in Bloomington, Indiana, reported to police that a group of 'zombies' attacked her in her Land Rover and covered the vehicle in 'purple goo'." —Wikipedia based on a Herald Times Online article

Imagine walking down a typical city street one day and seeing, in real life, a horde of zombies approaching you. Could it really happen? It has.

In 2001, promoters of a Sacramento, California, film festival organized a zombie parade. Although only a few people showed up, more and more every year have dressed as zombies and walked several blocks, groaning and crying out the famous line from *Return Of The Living Dead*, "brains... more brains..."

Mostly seen in North American and Australian cities, zombie walks have begun attracting hundreds or thousands of participants. One of the most popular ever was held at Monroevill Mall—the actual mall used in Romero's classic *Dawn Of The Dead*. Over 894 people dressed as zombies showed up, setting a Guinness World Record. The same event also raised money for the Greater Pittsburgh Community Food Bank.

Zombie walks have many alternative names: zombie mob, zombie march, zombie horde, zombie lurch, zombie shamble, zombie shuffle or zombie crawl. Some of the names are, by common usage, restricted to particular types of zombie walks. A zombie crawl, for example, usually refers to a zombie pub-crawl—a zombie walk that ends with beers at a local pub or pubs.

Although many zombie walks are held for fun, lately many have been used to sponsor charities or to raise public awareness. When the lack of an R18+ video game rating in Australia prevented the zombie game "Left 4 Dead 2" from being released in that country, over 170 people dressed as zombies and walked through the streets of Sydney. Several months later, the event was repeated with over 500 people dressed as zombies.

More common are zombie walks held for charity only. Many zombie walks support local or global food charities by collecting donations or actual cans of food. A 2008 zombie walk in Gran Rapids, Michigan, collected over 7,500 cans of food for a local food bank. Other charities supported by zombie walks include, "The Brain Foundation of Australia," anti-domestic violence groups, and a group that sends care packages to troops stationed abroad.

The zombie crawl or zombie pub-crawl has proven enormously popular. People dressed as zombies visit an area with several bars or pubs and go from one pub to the next all night long. Over 5,000 zombies attended the pub-crawl in Minneapolis in 2009.[xix]

Attending a zombie walk is not without risks. In 2006, an impatient driver attempted to drive his car thorough a crowd of zombies. After injuring several zombies, the usually docile zombie walkers fought back, resulting in severe damage to the car. Although so far no one has attempted to kill any zombie walkers, the fate of Bill Murray in *Zombieland* should encourage would-be zombies to be very careful about who they menace.

Conclusion

"When there's no more room in Hell.. The dead will walk the Earth!" — Teaser to Dawn Of The Dead

The public's appetite for zombies is near insatiable. Of the hundreds of zombie films made in the last 80 years, the majority were made during only the last 15 years — and the pace is accelerating. Successful zombie franchises show no sign of failing and major studies are bidding millions of dollars to adapt the latest zombie books, even enlisting movie stars like Brad Pitt and Natalie Portman who rarely do horror movies.

More than any other horror trope, zombies have been reinvented again and again. The merest hint of a zombie scares Haitians to this day, but when the Haitian legends stopped scaring American moviegoers, George Romero reinvented them as flesh-eating monsters risen from the dead by a mysterious force. When Romero's brain-dead, slow-moving zombies weren't scary enough, other writers sped them up and made them smarter.

When even fast zombies didn't scare audiences enough, the movie industry was quick to use zombies as common threat that brings characters together so they can make jokes and fall in love.

Where will zombies go next? If history repeats itself, within a few years newer, scarier, more violent, and more dangerous zombies will debut in a fairly-minor movie that goes on to achieve wild success. Perhaps the new zombies will premier in a video game, or a book, or a TV show.

But, wherever zombies are headed, we can be sure they aren't going back to the grave. Zombies are here to stay.

Top 10 Zombie Films

For Halloween 2007, the staff of Stylus magazine compiled an excellent list of the top 10 zombie films of all time. Just the titles are reproduced below:

1. *Dawn Of The Dead* (1978)

2. *28 Days Later* (2002)

3. *Day Of The Dead* (1985)

4. *Dead Alive* (1992)

5. *I Walked With A Zombie* (1943)

6. *Night Of The Living Dead* (1968)

7. *Return Of The Living Dead* (1985)

8. *Deathdream* (1974)

9. *Shaun Of The Dead* (2004)

10. *Pet Semetary* (1989)

About Minute Help

Minute Help Press is building a library of books for people with only minutes to spare. Follow @minutehelp on Twitter to receive the latest information about free and paid publications from Minute Help Press, or visit minutehelpguides.com.

[i] http://www.imdb.com/keyword/zombie/?titl e_type=feature&sort=release_date&start=301 Retrieved 15 March 2011

[ii] http://www.guardian.co.uk/books/2009/apr /09/austen-zombie-pride-prejudice Retrieved 15 March 2011

[iii] http://www.imdb.com/title/tt0816711/ Retrieved 15 March 2011

[iv] http://www.thefutoncritic.com/news/2010/1 1/08/amc-resurrects-the-walking-dead-for-a-second-season-639014/20101108amc01/ Retrieved 15 March 2010

[v] http://www.webster.edu/~corbetre/haiti/vo odoo/overview.htm Retrieved 15 March 2011

[vi] Commentary from *Night Of The Living Dead*, 2008 DVD edition, Region 1

[vii] *White Zombie: Anatomy Of A Horror Film* by Gard Don Rhodes. 2001, McFarland, ISBN 0786409886

[viii] http://www.stylusmagazine.com/articles/movie_review/stylus-magazines-top-10-zombie-films-of-all-time.htm Retrieved 15 March 2011

[ix] http://www.bloody-disgusting.com/news/15258 Retrieved 15 March 2011

[x] http://drcyclopsrecords.net/worldhorrornetwork/whn/?p=735 Retrieved 15 March 2011

[xi] http://rogerebert.suntimes.com/apps/pbcs.dll/article?AID=/19670105/REVIEWS/701050301/1023 Retrieved 15 March 2011

[xii] http://www.vanityfair.com/hollywood/features/2010/07/michael-jackson-thriller-201007?printable=true&currentPage=2 Retrieved 15 March 2011

[xiii] http://www.guinnessworldrecords.com/mediazone/pdfs/entertainment/061114_michael_j

ackson.pdf (PDF) Retrieved 15 March 2011

xiv http://www.mtv.com/news/articles/161653 7/thriller-set-overtake-eagles-topselling-lp.jhtml Retrieved 15 March 2011

xv *Handbook of Intellectual Property Claims and Remedies: 2004 Supplement*, Aspen Publishers, 2004

xvi http://www.paramuspost.com/article.php/2 0091026152024744 Retrieved 15 March 2011

xvii http://www.theeagleonline.com/scene/stor y/brooks-puts-brains-in-print-for-zombie-fanatics/ Retrieved 15 March 2011

xviii http://www.imdb.com/title/tt0365748/faq #.2.1.1 Retrieved 15 March 2011

xix http://www.mndaily.com/2009/10/11/zom bie-crawl-invades-cedar-riverside Retrieved 15 March 2011

9 781500 979379